IMAGINATION

Dedicated to Nance

DRAGON

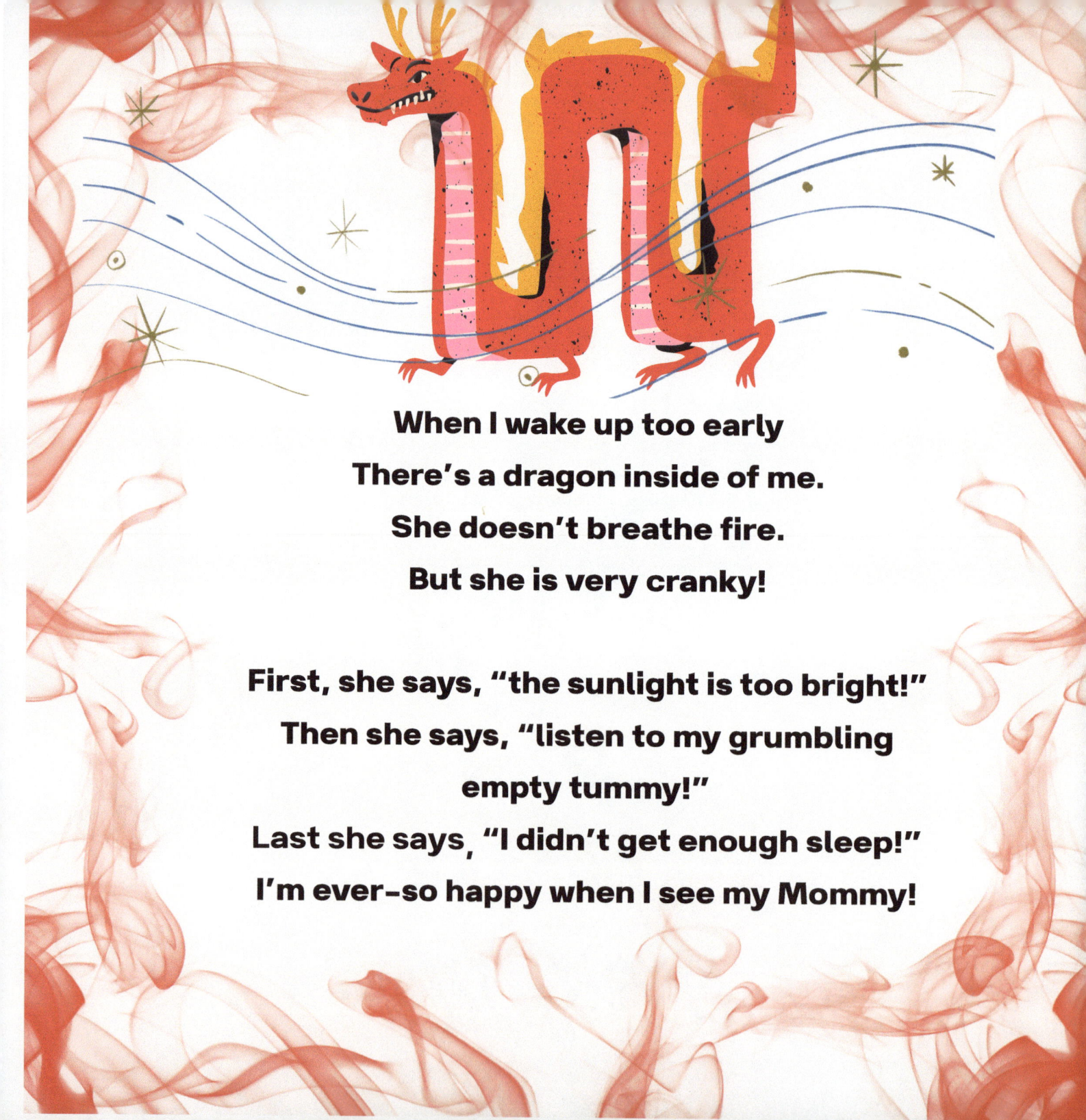

When I wake up too early

There's a dragon inside of me.

She doesn't breathe fire.

But she is very cranky!

First, she says, "the sunlight is too bright!"

Then she says, "listen to my grumbling
empty tummy!"

Last she says, "I didn't get enough sleep!"

I'm ever-so happy when I see my Mommy!

Then the dragon who lives inside of me...

Crumbles away when she hears Mommy's voice.

The dragon inside me, she yawns, and she stretches.

Mommy asks, "What do you want for breakfast?

Today is your choice!"

LION

When I can't fall asleep at night...
There's a lion inside of me.
'Go to sleep. Please.' I plead.
All he does is ROAR! And ROAR! And ROAR at me!

'Shhhh,' I say, 'Or you'll wake up Mommy and
Daddy!'
He ROARS and says, "You never stopped me
before!"
'Go to sleep. Pretty please!' I say.
All he does is ROAR! And ROAR! And ROAR!

And I know the lion inside of me is sad and scared.

He is tired and his roar is a sad, sad, plea.

It means he is feeling grumpy –
Sometimes he is JUST LIKE ME!

BLUE JAY

Sometimes when I'm too hungry.

There's a Blue Jay inside of me.

"Let's fly outside!" he sings.

"Outside is where I want to be!"

Mommy says, "Eat your dinner.

Then brush your teeth before bed."

The Blue Jay who lives inside of me

Says, "Let's go outside instead!"

So, I tuck a burger into my pocket.

Good thing I like it plain!

The minute we get outside.

It begins to thunder and rain.

The Blue Jay who lived inside of me

Decides to fly away.

I watch him fly across the sky.

And scoff my burger without delay!

When I'm having problems learning to ride my bike..

There's a chimpanzee inside of me.

"I learned to ride a bike in a circus," he brags.

He says he can teach me – "DEFINITELY!"

I cry because I've tried learning again and again.

He uses his hands to wipe away my tears.

"Give it another go!" he says.

"Soon it'll look like you've been riding for years!'

I think about it, while the other kids speed by.

I climb on board my bike, I pedal, and I steer.

The chimpanzee steadies me with his hands.

I pick up speed and switch gears!

WHEEEEEEEEEEEEEE EEEEEEEEEEEEEEEEEE!

CHAMELEON

When I sit alone at my new school
There is a chameleon inside of me.
She keeps turning me like a kaleidoscope.
The swirling colours camouflage me.

"You are very pretty!"
Says the chameleon inside of me.
"Thank you I say. Purple is my favourite."
"Purple is your colour," she says. "I agree."

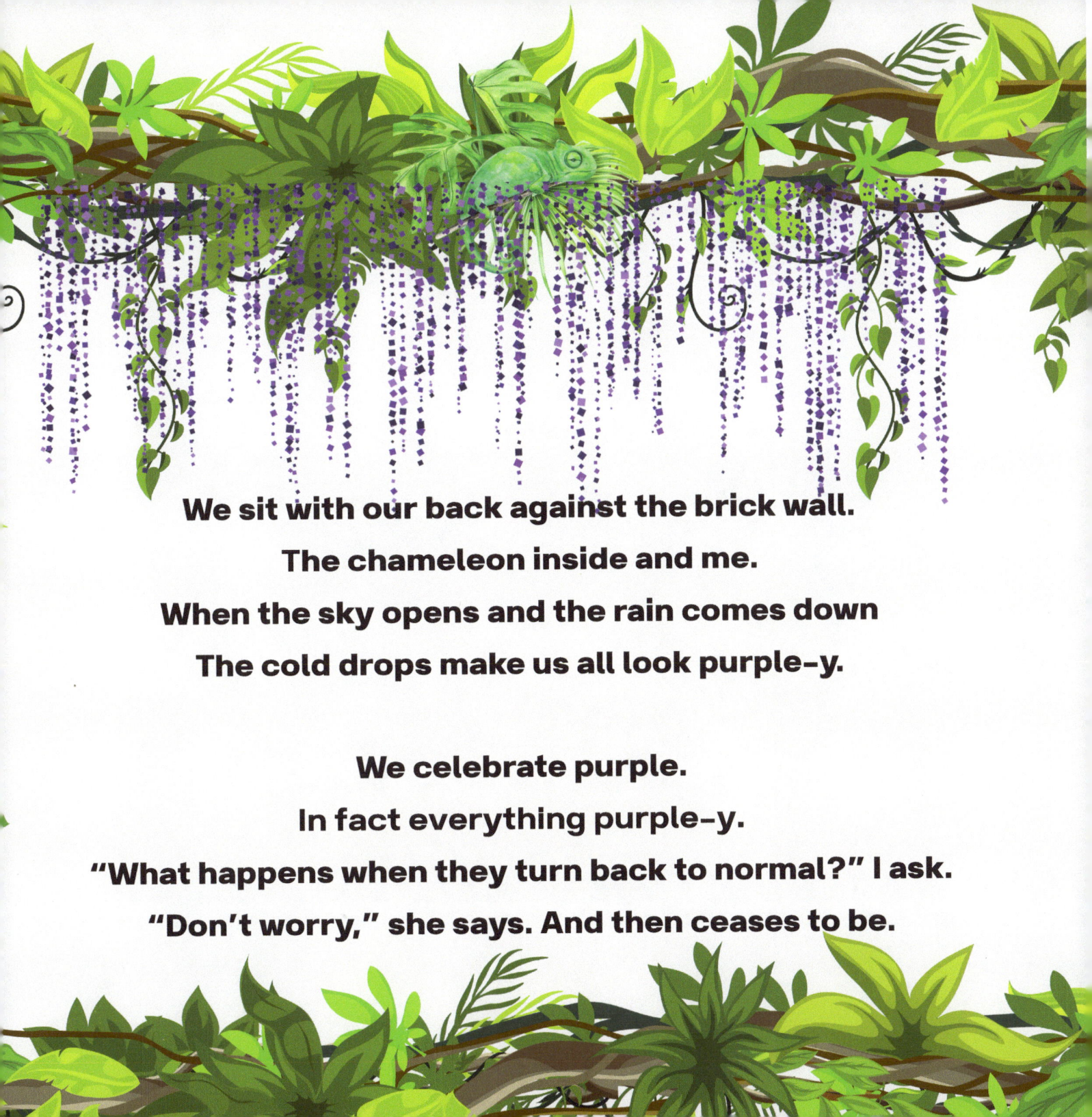

We sit with our back against the brick wall.

The chameleon inside and me.

When the sky opens and the rain comes down

The cold drops make us all look purple–y.

We celebrate purple.

In fact everything purple–y.

"What happens when they turn back to normal?" I ask.

"Don't worry," she says. And then ceases to be.

KOOKABURRA

When I can't stop laughing

There's a kookaburra laughing with me.

Her laugh is louder, and funnier.

And wakes up everybody!

I laugh along with the kookaburra.

My tummy hurts and I fall onto the floor.

Her kookaburra laughter rings out.

I laugh so much, I can't take it anymore.

"Go to sleep!" Daddy calls out.

"It's after 2 a.m.!" Mommy says.

The kookaburra lets loose with her song.

I'm laughing and in a daze!

Mommy and Daddy open the door.

They see me rolling with laughter on the floor.

The kookaburra looks at me, and I look at her.

And we don't feel like laughing any more.

GLOOM

When my mommy and daddy go out on a date night

There's a gloom inside of me.

The gloom drips doom down the walls

If I turned on the light, they wouldn't be.

But if I turned on the light

And the gloom went away.

I'd once again be alone in the dark...

With only the gloom inside of me.

.

The babysitter is downstairs (I'm not a baby!)
She is watching a little t.v.
While I'm up here all alone
With the gloom inside of me.

Then mommy and daddy are home!
And they run up to hug me!
The gloom in my room fades away...
No matter where they are – mommy and
daddy always love me!

BUTTERFLY

My best friend and I watch the others play.

In our wheelchairs we sit on the side.

She and I have butterflies inside us.

We giggle as they flutter and ride.

"Mommy says I am way too shy," she says.

I reply, "You can do anything if you try."

"All I want to do," she reveals,

"Is flit and flutter like a butterfly."

We hold hands and open our imaginations.

We are sailing on up to the sky.

The brakes on our chairs click OFF.

And we flit and flutter – best friend butterflies.

OWL

On the days I have trouble reading my ABCs
There is a wise owl inside of me.
He wears red-rimmed speckled glasses.
And he helps me to see what I cannot see.

"Reading and remembering, grow easier with time," he says.
And I know this to be true.
Still, when I'm behind the others and want to catch up –
The owl says, "You'll get there when the time is right for you."

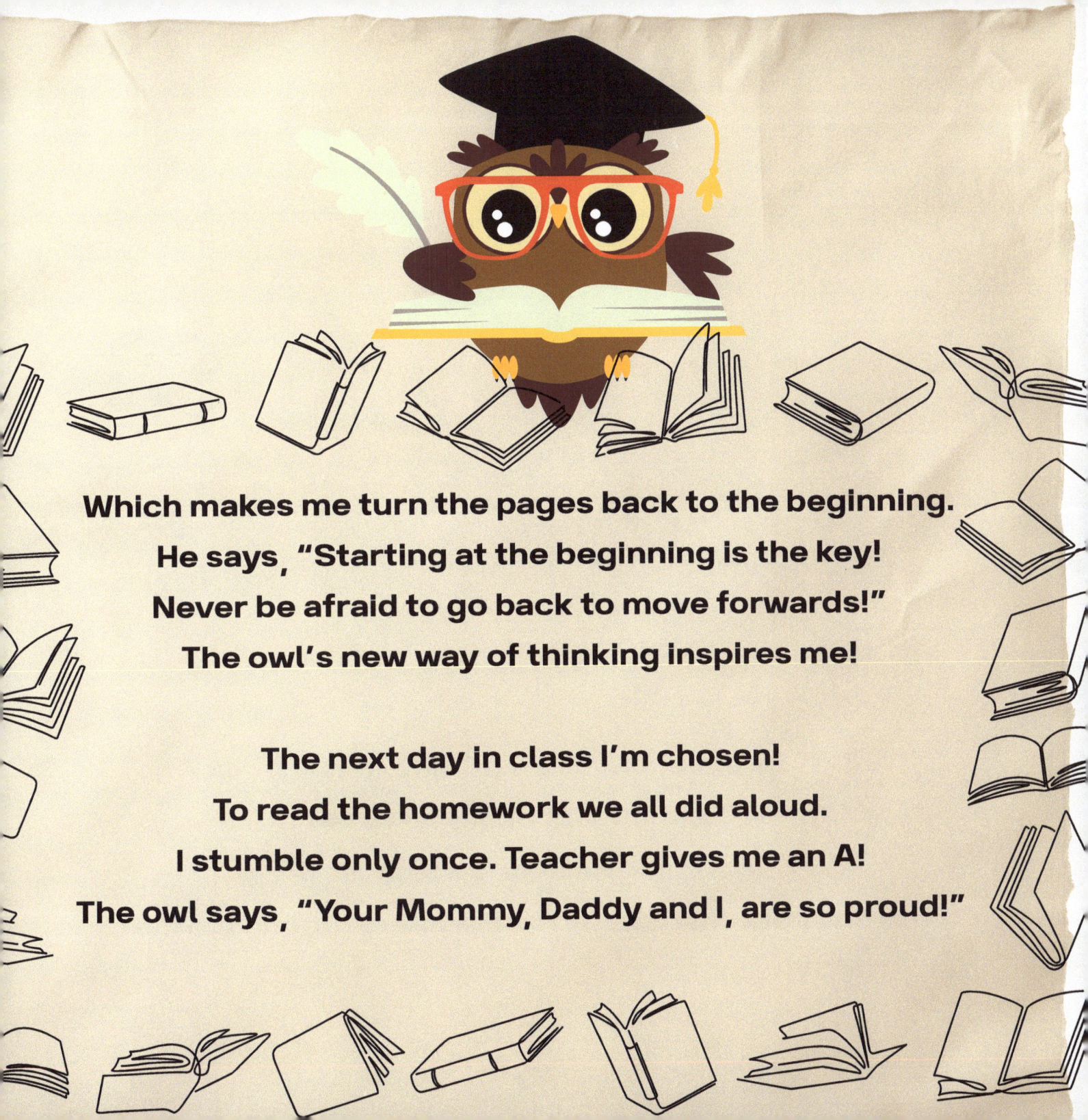

Which makes me turn the pages back to the beginning.

He says, "Starting at the beginning is the key!

Never be afraid to go back to move forwards!"

The owl's new way of thinking inspires me!

The next day in class I'm chosen!

To read the homework we all did aloud.

I stumble only once. Teacher gives me an A!

The owl says, "Your Mommy, Daddy and I, are so proud!"

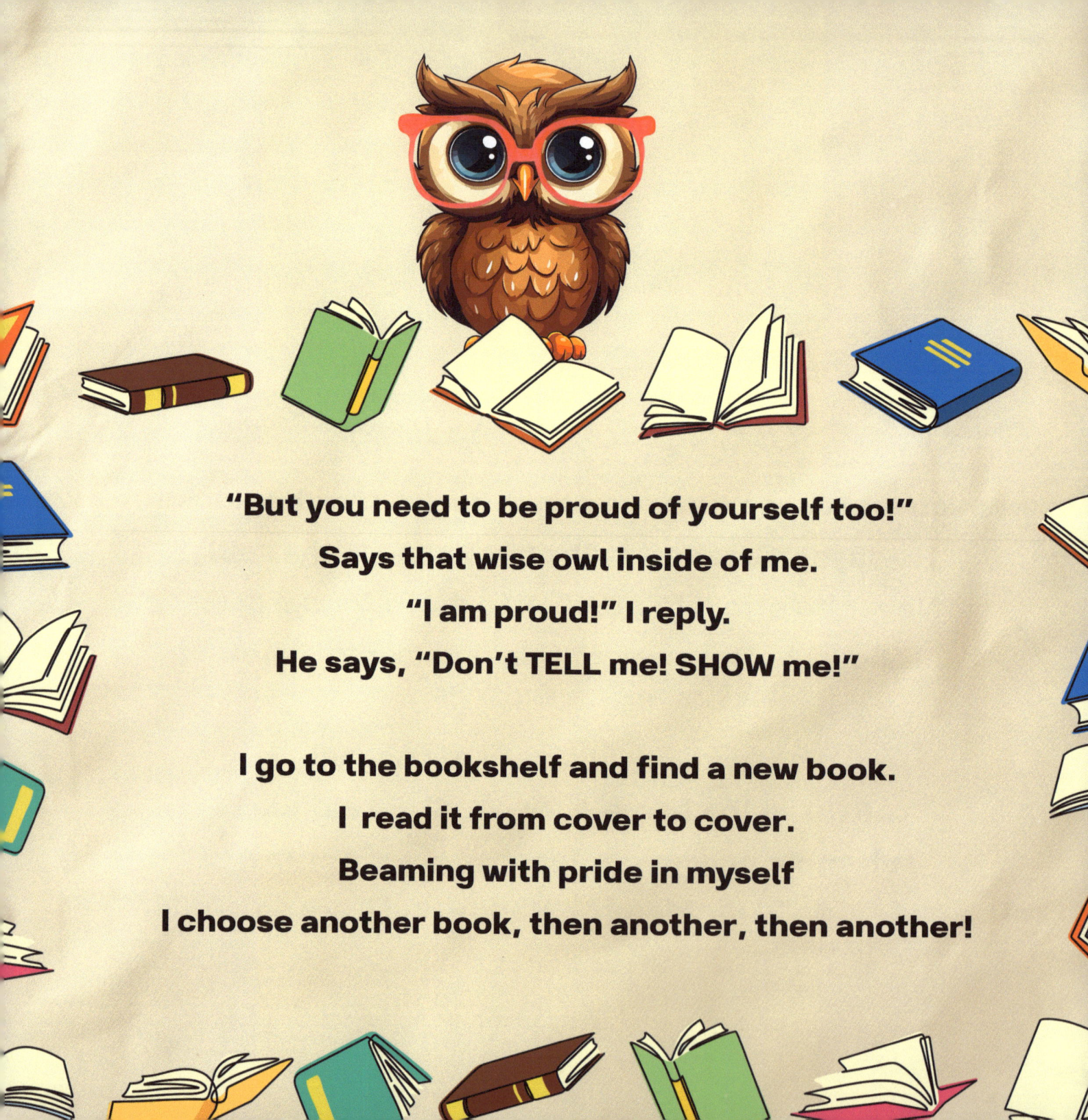

"But you need to be proud of yourself too!"

Says that wise owl inside of me.

"I am proud!" I reply.

He says, "Don't TELL me! SHOW me!"

I go to the bookshelf and find a new book.

I read it from cover to cover.

Beaming with pride in myself

I choose another book, then another, then another!

BEAVER

When I brush my teeth...
There's a beaver in the mirror looking back at me.
When I brush my teeth, he gnaws with his.
When I gargle, he points and laughs at me.

"My teeth are everlasting," he says.
I say, "You're lucky. My baby teeth will fall out soon."
"More reason to take care of your smile," he says.
"Your teeth to your smile, are like the sun is to the moon."

I grin a little, then go all in for a big smile.
The beaver smiles back at me with an impish grin.
"We're a dynamic duo!" he says.
And I agree with him.

HAMSTER

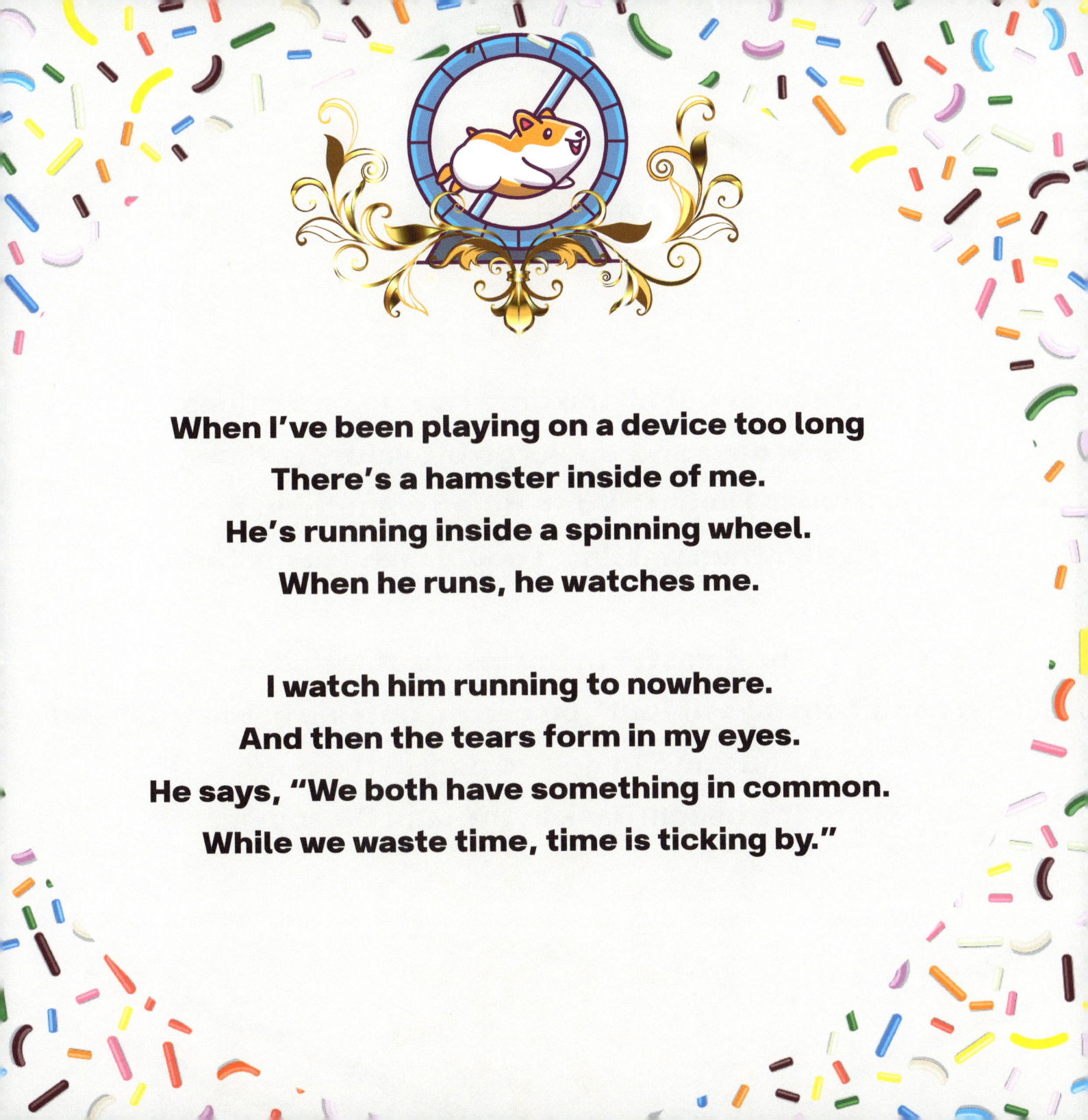

When I've been playing on a device too long
There's a hamster inside of me.
He's running inside a spinning wheel.
When he runs, he watches me.

I watch him running to nowhere.
And then the tears form in my eyes.
He says, "We both have something in common.
While we waste time, time is ticking by."

I think about all the time I waste on devices.

How days and weeks go by, valuable time.

When I could be out, doing something fun.

Rather than wasting, I could manage my time.

The hamster living inside of me says,

"I can't help myself, but you can go outside in the fresh air!

And you can go and play in the park!

Go to the beach! Bask in the sun! Go anywhere!"

I put down my device and take the hamster from his cage.

We open the front door and step outside. Outside we go!

We put our goggles and helmets on...

We get onto my bike and ride over hills high and low!

The hamster sits on the handlebars,

As we ride into the wind and scenery.

We say, "This is bigger, than bigger can be!"

Alone, but together we are FREE!

My sister is a super whiz in basketball.

She has a giraffe living inside of her.

I haven't reached my 'true height' yet.

But I'll grow some more soon, I'm sure.

I might get good at sporty things then.

For now, I have a bookworm living inside of me.

"Reading is your super-power!" she says.

"And your imagination is key."

Since I was little, I always ate up words.

To me they filled me up like food.

"Carrots a-plenty!" Mommy always says.

Thank goodness they taste so good!

GIRAFFE

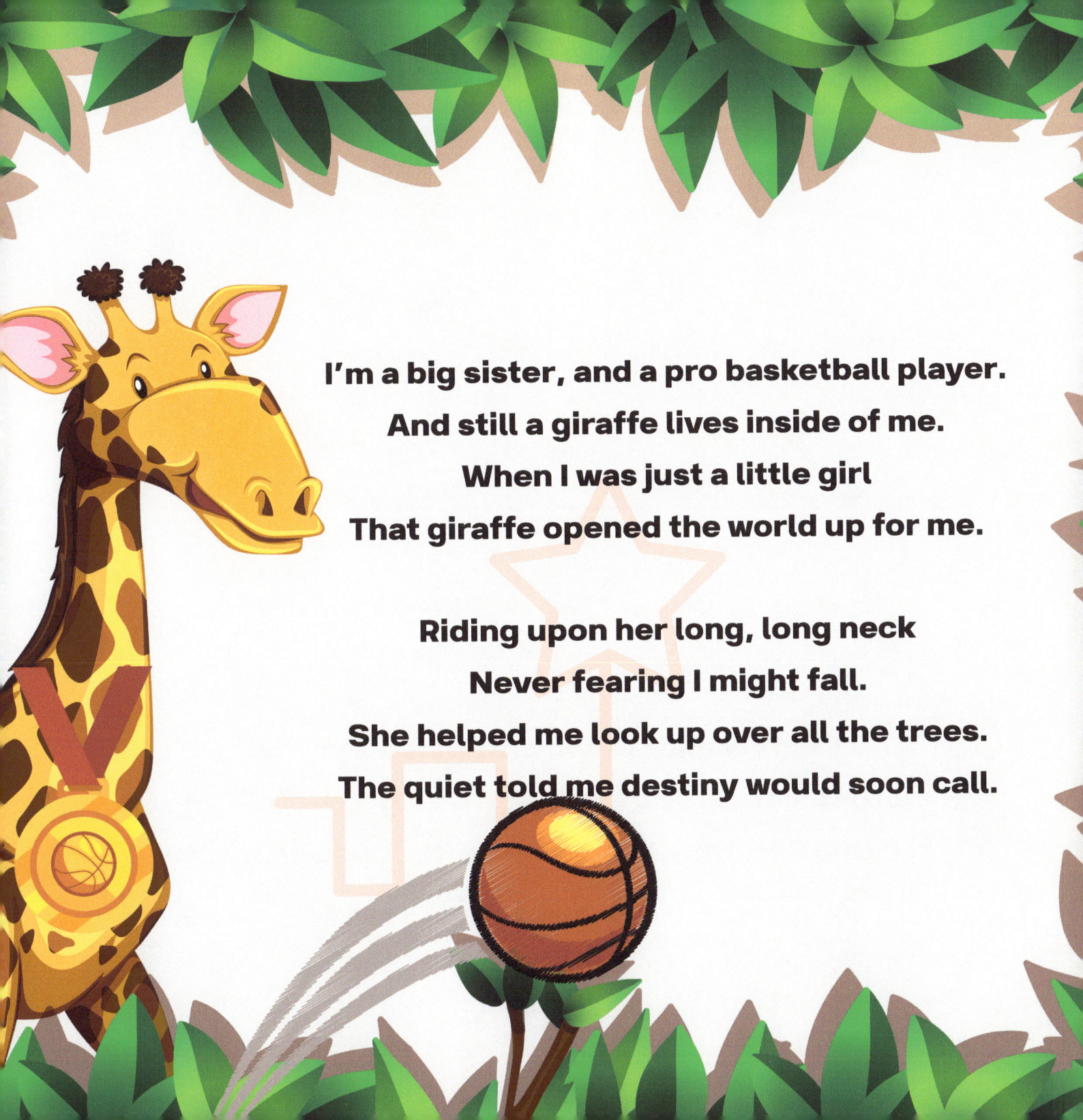

I'm a big sister, and a pro basketball player.

And still a giraffe lives inside of me.

When I was just a little girl

That giraffe opened the world up for me.

Riding upon her long, long neck

Never fearing I might fall.

She helped me look up over all the trees.

The quiet told me destiny would soon call.

I grew and I grew, and I grew very tall.

I learned basketball and loved being a shooting guard.

It came naturally to me; basketball was in my blood.

It was food for me, and I didn't even have to try too hard!

DOLPHIN

When I am in the pool, I take lessons to learn to swim.

And there's a dolphin leaping inside of me.

"You can do it!" he says, then he's off with a splash!

The water stings my eyes, and I can't see.

Next day when we have lessons, I discover goggles in my bag.

I put them on and wait for the teacher to begin.

Meanwhile I float, with my goggles under water.

There's no stinging! Lessons begin. WIN! WIN!

"Good thinking!" I say to the dolphin.

"Sure thing!" he replies.

Then he slaps his tail and giggles

As the water drops splash against my goggled eyes!

MOUNTAIN LION

When I climb up to the very top of the slide
A mountain lion is living inside of me.
"It's okay," he chides. "You're already halfway!"
The way down looks a long way off to me!

The slide itself reflects the bright sunlight.
I decide I'd rather be down there rather than up here.
The mountain lion wants to talk me down.
He says, "You can do it, my dear!"

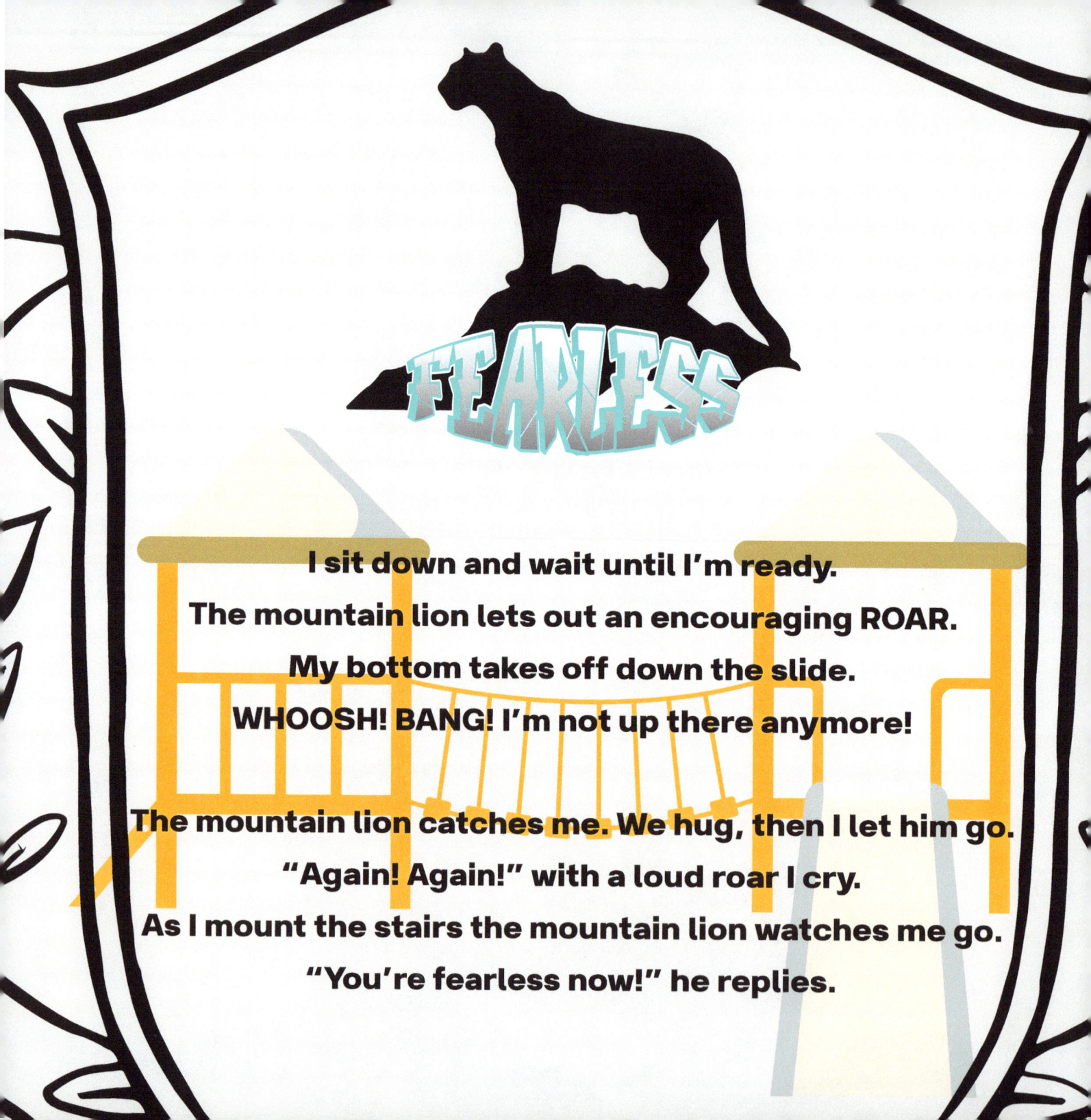

I sit down and wait until I'm ready.

The mountain lion lets out an encouraging ROAR.

My bottom takes off down the slide.

WHOOSH! BANG! I'm not up there anymore!

The mountain lion catches me. We hug, then I let him go.

"Again! Again!" with a loud roar I cry.

As I mount the stairs the mountain lion watches me go.

"You're fearless now!" he replies.

MY POEM